Unbroken Mind & Unspoken Words

Introduction

As a child, you see the world as a playground, full of wonder and smiling faces. You swing your anxious body from swings, embrace others with a warm heart and open arms. Your parents nurture you into the flower you are today, society breaks you down from the morals you walk in and lovers break your heart with no self-conscious. As we go through these phases of our life we take a piece of it with us; we may learn from our family mistakes, or become the mistake, we may break or rise above our pain. What life gives, you can sometimes be a mess, but your willingness to clean up the mess and put the pieces together will determine your survival.

From the periods of 2008-2015 I found myself in one heck of a phase, little did I know this phase was peculiar from other phases humans might face. This phase had connections, parallels, ups and downs. If I can give this phase a name it would be a Mathematical problem. But in my valley of breaking, bending, wheels of emotions, bullying, family curses, contemplation of death, failure and self-loathing I learned one thing in a nutshell 'I am who I am and no matter the lips that move swiftly say, I am who I am and God wants me to work with it.'

To my wonderful readers, my poetry is based on my experiences & experiences before my eyes. I want to inspire you. I want you to have an open heart and mind, feel what I felt.

To the readers who can relate to the experiences, you are brave and you are loved.

Stay Strong. Love Effortless. Be Kind. Share your story & Inspire.

Sincerely,

Sarah Oksana

There is poetry for every memory.

Sarah's Song

sing my song

a song so thousands of **Black Women** can hear the sweet melody

a melody that was once broken

but now found

a young **Black girl** didn't fit into the norms of a **Black Society**

they stood tall and told her she needs to portray herself "**Black**"

but she asked daily

"what is the portrait of **Black**"

her mama aint got the answers

her daddy barely spits a word

the stereotype we have created in our world for centuries

has become a punchline within our words

i've grown tired of the comments

time to elevate and take care of me

striving to be the woman I am within…

<u>Chapter 1: Leave It In The Waters</u>

fill my cup with love my mother never had

fill my cup with care my father never had

how can you fill a broken cup

how can you fill a cursed cup

the cup was passed to me

this tradition must come to an end.

breathe

wipe those tears

get up again

you have to be a strong **Black Woman.**

- *Note to self*

do you confront yourself

who are you when your luxury doesn't comfort the pain

who are you when you're standing in the emptiness

 broken and ashamed

you lift your fragile arms to the sky

your words hang heavily on your lips

and you ask God …why

help me.

there are **Broken Black Women**

i'm one of them

but it takes one bold **Black woman** to come forward

lay the pain, tears and screams down

one by one we bond over the pieces of what's left

together we realise we don't want this cup to be passed to our children

most of all we, don't want this cup for ourselves

a solution

yes

if only **Black brokenness** was this easy to resolve.

i love the taste of alcohol

it tangos on my tongue

soothes the pain

drowns inside my brain

I don't have to
think, feel, cry and scream

i smile and laugh

until the next day I remember again.

- *The Girl At 17*

this is me
there was a deeper issue that I didn't see
crush, please don't fall for her roses
the solution to my shattered esteem
handsome boy see beyond my darkened skin
i was ignorant to my history
i couldn't appreciate the gold.

it's a comedy
defined by other broken souls
it's sad
but they never drank the thought,
the broken souls paint me grey
there is something deeper than just fighting
words
i stood there and I was the star of the comedy
an earthquake of laughter shakes the pieces of
my soul
the expressions ripped through my esteem.

- *13 year old memory for a crush*

the mirror is my best friend
the mirror is my enemy, secretly
the mirror portrays an image pleasing to my
mother
the mirror portrays an image conflicting
society's' norm
too dark
oddly shaped nose
not enough hair
nappy
i hate the mirror
you are the devil
you made my teenage experience purely
insane.

maquillage it fits on my body like my skin
my mother wears it like a pageant queen
but I wasn't my mother's skin
i was cursed with my father's
here lies the unspoken issue
the issue **Black Women** face in the
community for centuries.

the white woman's product
spread across my cheeks
soft to the touch
it paints the pain pretty
the devil's mirror finds the problem
mama can never get my shade right
mama, I will never blame you
i hate those companies
when will they consider **Black Queens?**

- *14 year old first time with makeup*

they saw me
i was masked by the white woman's product
the comedy is back for a sequel
i won the Oscar
silently they find my experiment laughable
silly minds don't see the boiling issue
nobody has their eyes on
my own flesh and blood
blind!
they already drank from the cup.

welcome to the Wall of Fame
the audience in the jungle knows your fate
it's a damn shame
when I saw my name carved on the Wall of Fame
palpitations
river bank of tears
God's anger
what have I done
words have a strange way of bleeding within me…Hideous words
humans are the real monsters
what have I done
come forward…bully.

penny for your thoughts, bully
i will not sit and tell a press conference I'm A
Victim
honey pie you are the one I feel sad for
somewhere in your clouded judgment
you drank your own cursed cup
somewhere in your clouded judgment
you trusted someone who fractured you
come forward… bully.

jealousy
what an ugly trait!
imagine how disgusting it would be
if jealousy made up our bloodstreams
the biggest mistake
i watered my seed of jealousy
too much time was wasted being a wandering
eye
the fire in me was like no other
it was time to take an axe to the tree of
jealousy.

forgive you once, shame on me
forgive you twice, shame on me
forgive you thrice
another piece of me, you take
you have a collection of me hidden in your possession
do you ever stop and drink the thought
i'm hurting her
funny humans
we see the covers but not what's under the sheets.

i'm afraid of what love tastes like
it's been bitter for years
who would love me
what is there to love about me
my mind is the Civil War
don't love… it's painful
do love …you can't be lonely
don't love …it's a waste of time
do love … as a woman, you have to get
married
i see what other women don't see
the beauty is an illusion
there is a broken man
nothing is more misleading than a broken man
proclaiming love
it's a disaster
beware women.

i will never find love
the inner man haunts me day by day
how can two souls bond for centuries?

"Love is a decision." – *My Unbroken Mother*

oh, how the seasons change
my thoughts linger on the people that walked
in and out of my life
oh, how the seasons change
you walked into my life
that season changed
with open arms I embraced it with a smile
you have taught me
what I don't want for myself.

leaving behind the people and your feelings
to fulfill your purpose
this is one of the most difficult
nerve wrecking
decisions one will ever make.

time heals everything
a justification for the deeper issue
we depend on time to pass instead of a resolution
time passes and the hole get deeper
the deeper it gets we pacify it
time heals everything

let's have tea
i will sit in your deceitful company
your knife found its comfort within me
let me smile with you
you continuously laugh and drink with me
i see your collection of my blood
let me eat with you
but you have run out of places to cut me.

trust me, the lips of a beautiful monster pour onto me
hold my hand, I will guide you
to sacrifice myself for the vulnerable woman I am
trust me, the lips of a broken soul
you are my friend
a song the devil sings in our thoughts
trust me, the lips of an actor
we embrace each other for years
a justification so I won't see the destruction.

TRUST
a five letter deceiving word
we love to rehearse it to perfection
beautiful leach, you need an Oscar
trust me
i have to trust myself before I trust you
trust leaves the door open for vulnerability
how quickly I got hurt by the lips of the trust-
ee.

i want to sit in the waters of every woman that
was rejected
i love you and God loves you
sorry isn't enough
i can't imagine how heavy it feels
you gave yourself exhaustively, for what
to sit in your river of tears with an empty soul
for what,
to find yourself between the walls of a painful
reality
for what,
confused in the mind at your mistakes
you have mastered the art of self-loathing
maybe it's my fault
this is what rejection feels like.

the artist is a trickster
he has painted the portrait
it is ready for display
you only see yourself to blame
but I'm not falling for the foolery
honey pie, your names are written in black
every crime, you have committed against my soul
time is up, come forward and turn yourself in
this is what it feels like not to blame yourself for another's sins.

what a disgusting story to indulge in
my body feels like a ball of fire
how tragic it is for a woman to carry her
mother's rejection for years
she's 50, half of her life she carried this cup
to my mother, sorry isn't enough
you are loved by me
you are loved by God
you are not a mistake
you are not a burden
your happiness isn't fractured
to my mother, you don't have to carry the cup
this is what it feels like to release yourself from
their sins.

to the girl who loves to use her words to scar
i laugh
how quickly you compose your tune,
when you face the music
how bold you aren't.

to the girl with her skin like milk
hair dripping with her sins
you define everyone
but failed to see your mirror is reflecting
what an ugly human.

it is a disgraceful trait
spitting small-minded words
"she's a nobody"
as she laughed like the devil
never let someone like me
stand behind you
i see your true colors
it's oozing
i wonder what hateful words are said in secret
from the lips of this 'she devil'.

she makes me sad
her cup is broken
she makes me sad
her justification is to be a bull
she makes me sad
her lies are her truths
she makes me sad
her beauty will fade
but this disgraceful trait will remain.

i love the eyes God has given me
not physically
spiritually
i see things little girls don't see
i quickly distant myself from strange beings
your soul is poisonous
maybe it's your actions
it doesn't pattern your words
i'm scared
anyone that says walk
but runs, is someone that needs to be under a microscope
this is how my loneliness start.

my mornings brought me joy
but my nights brought me sadness
my mind was a Civil War of overbearing
thoughts
God and the Devil faced each other on my
battlefield
i made my bed of tears, silently
my own solution
my own comfort in the dark times
you only know how I feel
when you walk the valley with me.

there isn't a name for this cup
it's been a burden for 2 years
the comforting sounds of my tears filled the air
the season change and my emotional roller
coaster remain the same
they don't teach you whatever this emotion is
in my culture
in my Blackness,
a black woman is taught to be independent
be educated
find a good man
get married
have kids
love God
but what about the cracks of your humanity
where's the solution
no, honey pie
just get over yourself
you got to let that go
no one wants a sap of a human in their
company
i don't know if this makes me better or worse.

black history is apart of me
as my fingers rip through the pages of the past
a mixture of power and sadness haunt me
but something will stick with me forever
Malcolm X has taught me
black women are the most disrespected
this will never be okay
over 50 years later the cracks of our history are leaking.

our black men love to belittle us
this was a hobby, now its history
shockingly
Black Women
you are accepting your role in the man's play
for what?
you bear his children and keep his house in
peace
we have forgotten how powerful we are
how can you forget Miss Rosa
how can you forget Miss Coretta
how can you forget Miss Nina
our men enjoy manipulating us to be on
battlefield with each other
how can we allow our minds to be altered for
the man?

let me weep
for the **Black women** handling their mental
stability the way society taught us
let me weep
for the **Black women** who take care of your
children, her children and no one's children
let me weep
for the **Black women** that have fallen to the
throne of the man
she's in fear, but no one hears her
let me weep
for the **Black women** whose bodies were
sacrificed
our men will never understand the pain
let me weep
for the **Black women** who were forced to eat
out of the plate of injustice
let me weep
for the **Black women** who lay down in their
graves and swallowed the injustice
it was a bitter pill.

black bodies are falling everyday
justice has fallen
who do we turn to
when our help is our enemy
if no one remembers their name
i do
I stand for them.

let us hold each other in times of darkness
my Black Brothers and Sisters
this race isn't over
justice will be served
success will be achieved
every hurdle we face we shall jump
every man that stands up against us we shall defeat
we shall lift our hands to the Lord
tears of joy will fill our cup.

don't tear each other down
this is their psychology
violence will never be the solution
this is their victory
educate yourself
this is what they fear
remember your history
this will bring them to your feet.

we walk on the line of life
as we try to balance on the line
our experiences become our classrooms
we learn from every wound that was left open
she doesn't like to show the scars
it could have happened, but it didn't
the thought still lingers loosely, what if
she hasn't forgotten how his fingers danced on
her body
he was stranger inviting himself in
an evil energy struck her from a Godly man
before the worst
she was released
no one saw the scars
Her, God and Her.

i don't know what scares me the most,
the venom of snakes or
the tongues of men
the unbearable feeling of their company scares me
i panic
please don't leave me alone!
for me, it's a trigger
my mind wanders to the twisted possibilities of
standing alone with a man
the scars made me numb to love
the cup I drank taught me this.

your daughter
your wife
your sister
they are victims
but are being stoned
close your legs
turn your cheek
cover your body
maybe the man will respect man if you do
how quickly have we forgotten where respect starts?
in the home.

for the millions of girls and women who sat in
silence
your bruises tell the stories
your tongues can't
for many years you served at his feet
everyone was looking behind the curtains
but no one saw you
for many years you learned the art of masking
the pain
you became an artist
for many years you wound yourself
he allowed you to self-blame
i see you!
i see you finally got up
dust your knees
washed the blood off your hands
wiped those tears
time's up!

you will face the mirror again
he is your friend
he is your lover
he is your enemy
you had a marathon for too long
time to face the reflection
whether you're 21 or 40
this is your moment
you have the power to define yourself to him
this is your moment
you have the power to tell him goodbye
this your moment
you have the power to stand up to him
this is what self-worthy feels like.

i love my skin
i love the way it clothe my bones
what a spectacular event!
i love the way the sun kisses my skin
and the rain glistens on my blackness
my creator is a chef
he created a Goddess
a **Black Queen**
what a recipe!
he spent nine months baking me to perfection
21 years later he is admiring me
he appreciates the art
this is what self-worth taste like.

our feet and hearts will make a joyful sound
every woman of every color
we lift our voices for the skies
freedom isn't won with silence
equality isn't won with silence
our demands are as loud as our voices
the time is now.

i would like to believe I can heal the world
i would cut the flesh of every soul
i wish they can see,
every soul bleeds the same
but it is not my job to heal the world
every soul has a job to deliver themselves from ignorance
it is a step to the healing process.

never allow your enemy to be seated behind
you
they will strike you at the weakest moment
i placed my feet in the enemy's shoes,
it is my time to strike.

a day will come when I will make you eat my
words
you will choke on what I felt all those years
the tables will turn
and the season will change
i will collect your blood and tears in my
possession
i will be the one holding the knife
and you will be the one spitting my words
this is what avenging my soul feels like.

no more felonies against my body
rehabilitate and rise again.

blood is thicker than water

family ties are unbreakable
fairytales mothers tell their little one
we are not like the families in the picture
frames
the blood of my family is thick
the thicker the blood, the deeper the faces of
betrayal reveals itself
she holds her head up embracing her offspring
her bloodline swam to the river and never
looked back
the ties they speak of are lies
blood is tainted.

black roses grew bountiful in our garden
the thorns signify our rebirth
we are fierce
the leaves grew green like our hearts
every hurricane that hit us
our heads, hearts and souls were the armor
to my mother
your bloodline is selfish and cruel
but my loving mother
we never needed our bloodline to cover our
backs.

to my mother's bloodline
the way your limbs danced
there aren't anymore words left,
my gratitude to you.

words are deceiving, the eyes tell the truth

if only they can read my eyes

i'm perfecting smiling the pain

there is something lurking in the waters
as I sat on the edge and stare at my reflection
i see my strengths and weaknesses
i was born in these waters
i can either choose to swim or drown
this is what the water gave me.

<u>Chapter 2: Thoughts for Father</u>

*Fathers, be good to your daughters
Daughters will love like you do – John Mayer*

there's an underlying problem with humans
our tongues speak
before our eyes read the chapter.

i will say what I have to say
until my last breath
Black women!
we were silenced for too long.

i can change my clothes
i can change my company
i can change my thoughts
but I can't change daddy.

my thoughts drift away
i like to imagine,
what would I say at my father's funeral
would I lay him down a bed of roses
would I pour him a glass of whiskey
would he appreciate me now that he is dead?

would I cry after he dies
i wasted two years of tears on him when he
was alive
if I cry at my father's funeral,
i would cry because I was finally free.

there are **Broken Black Women**
the audience calls her "whore"
this becomes her name
but there is a deeper issue
for she is a fatherless creature
she spent her life
trapped in the fallacy of what a man's love is
she lingers, then leaves
she lingers, then leaves
the audience shouts "whore"
they are blind.

i see the pattern
i dream not to walk the path of this kind of
woman
i don't want to live from sheet to sheet
skin to skin
i want my temple to be sacred and respected
i do not want to drink from this tainted cup.

the first man's duty was to shower me with
love
he mentally destroyed me
he showed me the many faces of men
quickly I learned what kind of man I don't
want for myself
quickly I learned what kind of man I don't
want for my children.

i will forget the insults from the lips of humans
i will forget the gifts of a Trojan horse
i will never forget the day my father faced me
the fire in his eyes was a glimpse of what hell
looked like
his tongue was soaked with his bitter thoughts
he had compared me to the women who sell
their bodies for a coin.

the words of my father is the winter of my
body
but it wasn't his words,
it's his expression from head to toe
his eyes like Satan's favorite demon
he sat staring at me
my eyes was the sea
his long stares bothered me
he is a sociopath
he treats me like a stranger,
crushing me was his ideology of revenge on
my mother.

i will tell you a secret
it is the most difficult, but unbelievable secret
the most wicked people I have encountered
are,
my father
my mother's mother
the cup they drank it was poisonous
it became apart of their bloodstreams.

i can see you sitting
spitting words at me
what a bad seed
what a disrespectful child
yes! I am indeed
i am a Scorpio
it is written in my stars
but I don't believe in stars
i believe in truth
your opinions mean nothing
you didn't walk the valley with me.

a polygraph for deception is in the company of
my mother's mother
i need salvation to sit in the company of my
father
this is not something little girls say out loud
but papa and grandma, I'm not a little girl
anymore.

i left you that blank page
you needed to exhale, honey pie....

many nights I sat drenched in my tears
i blamed myself for a man's crime
how familiar it sounds
a **Black Woman** taking the burdens of a black man sin
i would kiss my hands, but it was numb
he touched me and I was scarred
he trick me into drinking from the cup
how can I trust a man again
the man is silent
i'm the one to blame,
blame the **Black Woman**.

the choir sings my name,
light a candle and pray for my pain
the wings of angels embrace me
my soul resurrected from my body
i was lifeless,
how weak the black man made me
the world finally got to look behind the
curtains,
it is a sad day for the fatherless girl
she is a pity party, she is a cry baby and she is a
drama queen
dear audience the first man to love me
destroyed me
you don't get to have the last words.

we both need therapy, father
someone destroyed you, your cup
you destroyed me, my cup
i don't want to destroy my children.

my mother and her pacifying words
it guides me
but troubles me, it's like an illusion
we are fine, we don't mind, we don't worry
about it
dear mother don't speak perfection for me
this is a mess
i want you to know what the black man did to
me
it is a lesson
it is a chapter
it is my journey
let me grieve
this is my truth.

the darkness was my company
i caught my tears
for many moons, I cried
my heart was frozen
no man can move my emotions
i wasted it on my first love.

the foolish part of storm
i could've sheltered somewhere safer
but I stayed
a part of me wanted him to know me
a part of me wanted him to love me
but how can a man who has never tasted love,
appreciate its beauty.

it is a dream of dying peacefully by the hands
of nature
i dream of dying peacefully by my own hands
it would've been a masterpiece
this will go down in history,
to see a blade pierced gracefully in me
the orchestra plays my tune loudly
it would've been a relief
to see my statue drenched in blood
the pain
anger
rejection
bullies
heartbreakers
leaches
oozing through my veins, every gallon of
blood tells the stories
my last words,
would anyone care?

the joys of death completes me
i don't have to think about how fragile my first
love made me
i don't have to feel like I failed everyone
my own blood soothes me
i am finally free.

but I don't want to die by my own hands
my hands were made to create
my hands were made to love
my hands were made to embrace my purpose
my hands were not made to hold a knife to my
temple
i want to live.

i can't imagine the train of emotions,
for mothers to lose their little ones by their
own hands
my heart floats with you
the agony that led you to this moment, little
one
it is not your fault
a monster in your life was destructive
a monster in your life was a coward
a monster in your life didn't see he was your
pain
little one, let the angels guide you home
mama will remember you for your smiles.

i cannot fix my fathers' sins

but I can make sure it doesn't become a part of me.

i can sit on my bed
and write thousands
millions
billions
of words
saying it out loud would not sound nor feel the same.

it is time, mother
time for us to dust our skirts
lick our wounds
bathe in the river of blessings
cleanse our life from their sins
the world is the audience and they have a
passion for opinions
but only you see your wounds, mother
and I only see mine.

Chapter 3: The Final Thoughts

forgiveness is apart of me
the Gods in the sky
the crowds in the stand
they have hope for me to forgive,
in my ungodly hour
i question my father's worth of forgiveness
is it something I extend to him
would forgiveness take back his vile words
if I don't forgive, I'm lifting an eternal weight
if I do forgive, there isn't justice.

when you think of St. Tropez
you think of my heart
it is a summer afternoon by the sea
it floats on the waters
quenching you thirst with champagne
a heart like St. Tropez can never turn away
from the door of forgiveness
a heart like St. Tropez sails its way to the
enemy's door and smiles
here is my glass of forgiveness
drink with me.

caressing anger is a death trap to one's self
imagine wearing anger like a favourite pair of
jeans
it clings to your body and follows you
angry for what
he buried you and never looked back
you were breathing
you fought your way back to reality
the lesson you learned was anger
it blinds you from seeing you survived.

i am a human being
every mistake is a lesson
my mistakes will never become a pattern
i will nurture my children
they will not cross the line of my mistakes
they will not get a glimpse of this cup
it was tainted.

if I allow my heart to be broken twice
i am my mother's child
if I open my ears to the stories
my heart is sealed
if a man is strong enough to break the seal
he must be a gift from God.

for the boy who left his heart open loosely
your rejection made me wiser
for the boy whose words pull me into the sea
your lies made me stronger
for the boy whose eyes lingers on me like a stranger
a day will come when you hear my name
and comfort yourself in regret
for the boy whose actions didn't pattern his promises
your breaches taught me to walk away with a smile.

i am the light
the blessing from my mother's womb
and a burden to my father
God speaks in my dreams
how often do I hear
he doesn't want me to fear humans
he wants me to keep my eyes on the light
he doesn't want to pick my body from the river
he wants me to bathe in the river of forgiveness
he wants me to forgive my father.

they have taught me, actions are more credible
than words
the way their limbs dance
taught me it was time to end the show.

Black Women
our hearts break
our bones snap
but we rise again
our comebacks are immortalized.

we turn to religion in times of darkness
but the men in our religion are the darkness
they violate the vulnerable
they call themselves the voice of the Gods
it is a board game
he is the ringleader
he rolls the dice
he found another victim for his game.

karma
it is dangerously beautiful
you sat on your throne for centuries
you placed your feet on the heads of your victims
karma is graceful, but deadly
its strings pull you gently off the throne
your hands and feet kiss the floors of karma
the higher your throne the harder you fall
your tears are the signal for your victim's victory
you were struck by karma.

this is my kingdom
i fix my hair
i'm covered in the finest garments
it compliments my skin
the wine is being poured
the food is bountiful
i grace their presence
the Queen has arrived
years of self-doubt
she has finally fallen in love with herself.

i will not allow you to kiss my hands
i will not allow you to drink from my waters
i will not allow you to touch my open heart
i am not God
your chances are expired
you ran me dry
it took years to end my drought
this isn't goodbye, honey pie
this is thank you, lesson learned.

i question the world's intentions
if my hair was straight
my smiles were wide
my skin wasn't like midnight
my fabric had a higher taste
would there be stories to tell?

be the voice for hundreds of women
who are still drowning in their silence.

-Young Black Feminist

i am not an item
to be viewed behind a glass
you cant buy me with paper nor cheap words
my love is like the Egyptian Goddess of life
it is royal and sacred
you see my hair, eyes and smiles
the beauty fools the male minds
Black Women are not facile
the audience laugh because I never make a choice
my mind can never be simple
why should I take a teaspoon
when I deserve a cup

i convinced myself
if my smiles were intimidating
my body isn't welcoming
if my eyes were the deepest parts of hell
no man would have thoughts of me
these are the side effects of what I have
learned

it is a punchline among friends
men are not the dish on my plate
i smile but I'm not a joke
my mother calls it a phase
she spends the day justifying my disease
for those who laugh never ask the story
a summer evening behind a stranger's door
the fear that glazed across my skin
the prayers I quietly said to be released
maybe it was the way my father raised me
with an angry spirit and bitter words
it taught me well, jokes on me
this is a penny for your thoughts next time you laugh.

i will love you until the sun ceases its existence

and the moon dims it shine

remember my unspoken words in your times of despair.

release the baggage from the past.

Printed in Great Britain
by Amazon